Whose house?

JEANNETTE ROWE

SOUTHWOOD
BOOKS

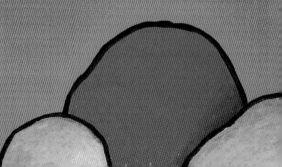

Whose house?

Whose house?

Whose house?

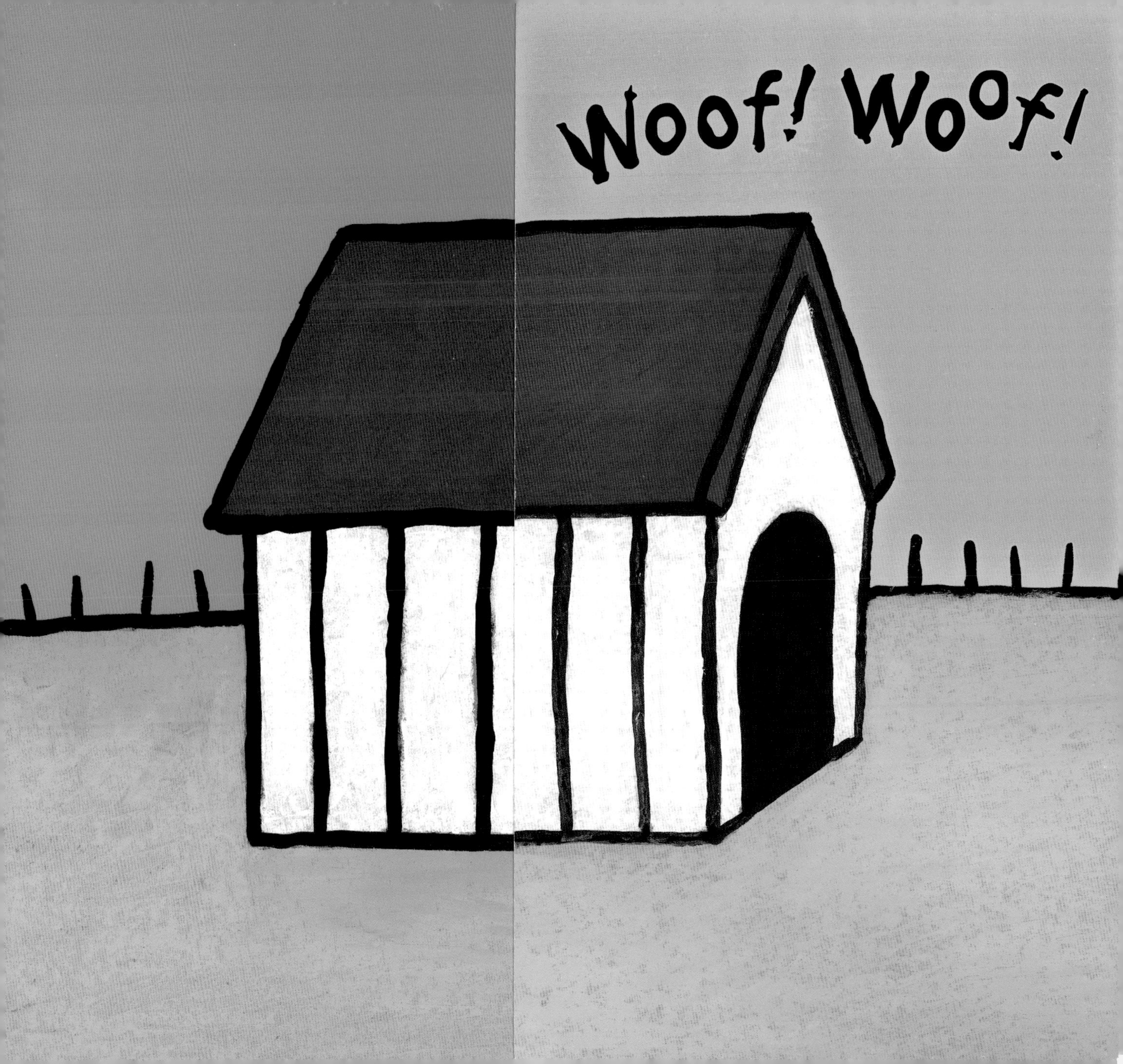
Woof! Woof!

Whose house?

Whose house?

Whose house?

Twitch! Twitch!

Whose house?

MY HOUSE!

For Darcy and Matilda

First published 2001 by Southwood Books Ltd.,
4 Southwood Lawn Road, London, N6 5SF
Originally published by ABC Books for the
Australian Broadcasting Corporation
GPO Box 9994 Sydney NSW 2001

Copyright© Jeannette Rowe 2001

ISBN 1 903 207 25 8

A CIP Catalogue record for this book is available
from the British Library.

The illustrations were drawn with oil pastels on coloured paper.
Designed and typeset by Monkeyfish, Sydney, Australia
Colour separations by PageSet Pty Ltd, Australia
Printed in Hong Kong Quality Printing.